# Forests and its animals

Copyright © 2023  coloring book
ISBN: 9798857796580
Relaxing and educational book about forests and animals

For more information:
Márcio C. Renner
mrenner77@gmail.com

The author is passionate about nature, art and culture.

He took the opportunity not only to have a hobby of painting animals, but also to bring more information about their habitats.

There will be many moments of joy and knowledge.

Have fun!!!

See also another book by the author

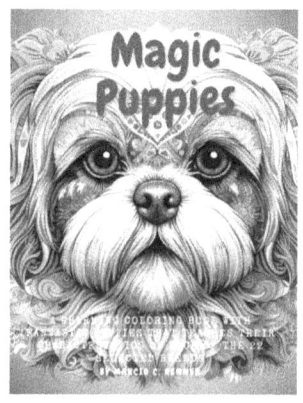

# This book is being colored by the artist:

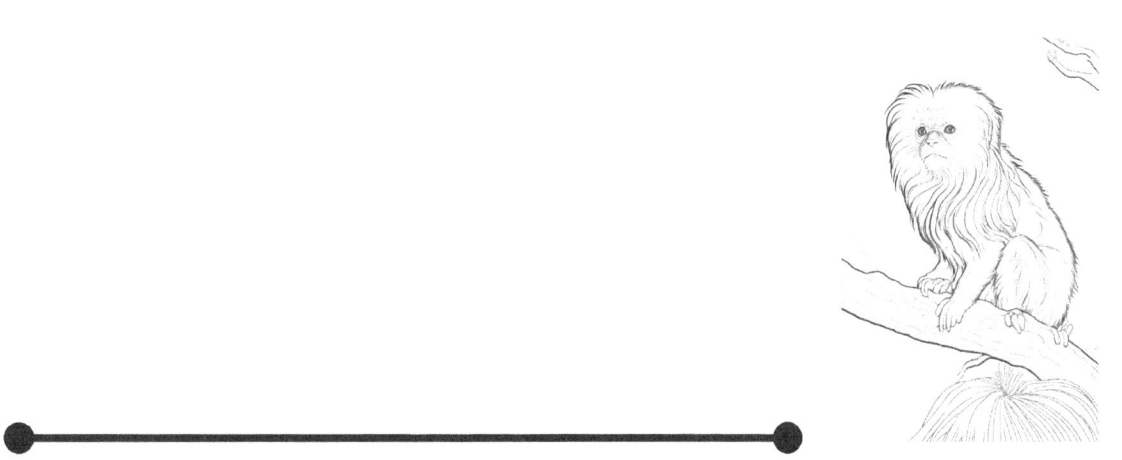

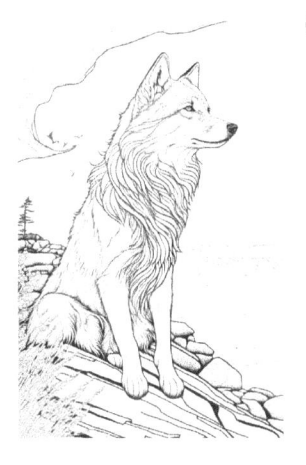

# Tropical forest

It is a type of phytogeographic domain characterized by receiving a large amount of rainfall and presenting high levels of biodiversity and evapotranspiration. Humidity and high temperatures are the main characteristics of tropical forests. They are biomes with greater productivity and variety of species on the planet. They are also called tropical rain forest or humid forest because of the high rainfall of the regions where they are located. They receive this denomination because they are located between the tropics of Cancer and Capricorn.

The main characteristics of tropical forests are: the presence of tall trees, the warm climate and the high precipitation. The average temperature reaches 20 °C and it rains about 1,200 millimeters annually.

Despite supporting a huge variety of plants, the soils of tropical forests are poor. Its productivity is guaranteed by the great availability of water and high temperature. In addition, the necessary nutrients are found mostly in the biomass of the living trees themselves than in the soil.

The process of decomposition of organic matter is extremely fast in tropical forests and this is what ensures the cycling of nutrients.

# Golden Lion Tamarin

He lives exclusively in the Brazilian Atlantic Forest, in the state of Rio de Janeiro.
The Golden Lion Tamarin is an animal threatened with extinction for a long time because of the destruction of its habitat, its survival is due to projects and conservation units.
It is a mammal, whose length can vary between 27 and 30 cm, its syrup can measure up to 40 cm in length and its weight is between 350 g to 800 g.

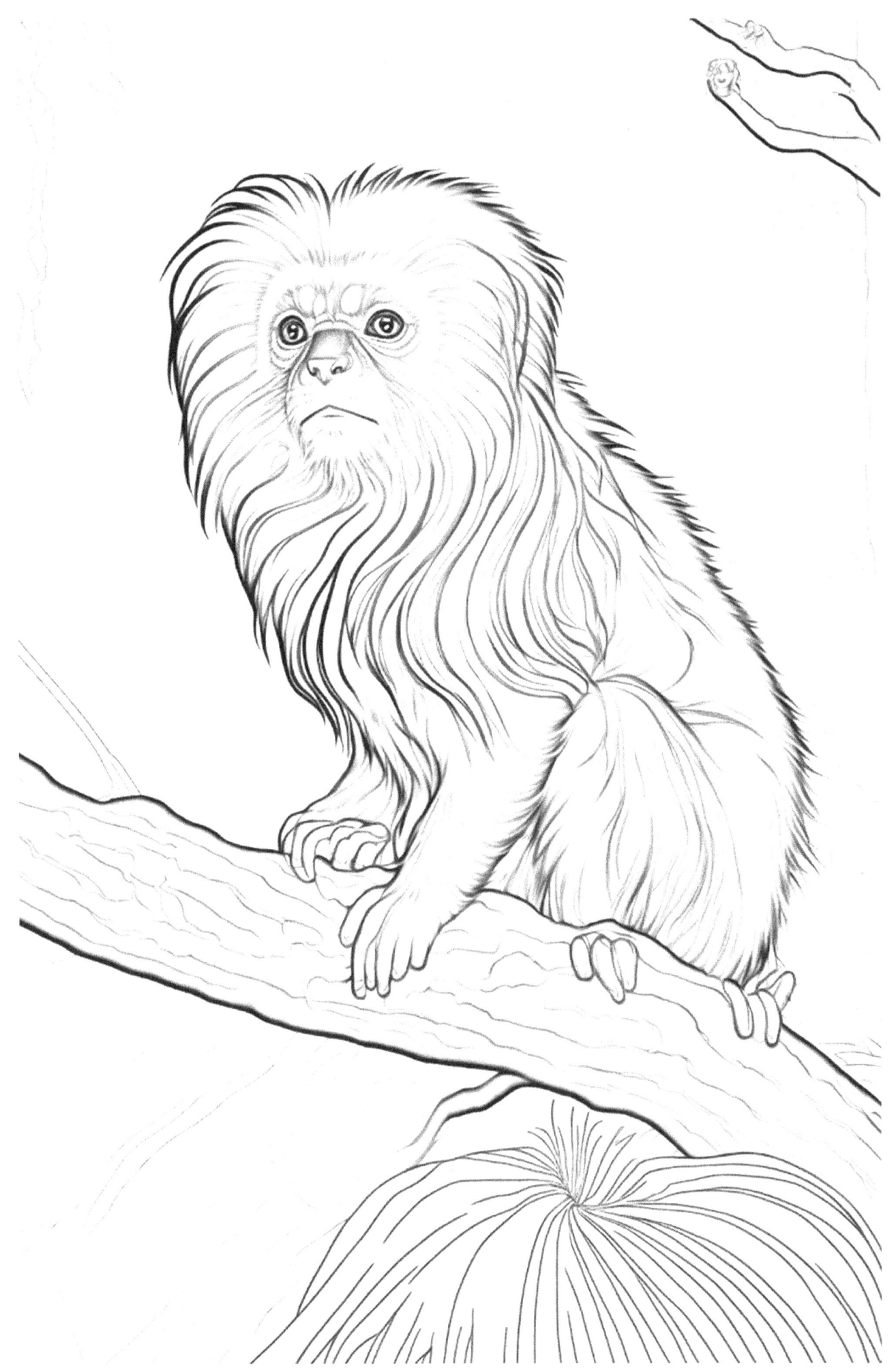

# Jaguar

The jaguar, is a big cat native to the Americas. It is the third largest cat in the world - after the tiger and lion - the largest in the Americas.

It is a carnivorous animal that feeds on a variety of prey, including deer, monkeys, birds, fish, and smaller mammals.

The jaguar is a top predator and plays an important role in maintaining the balance of its ecosystem.

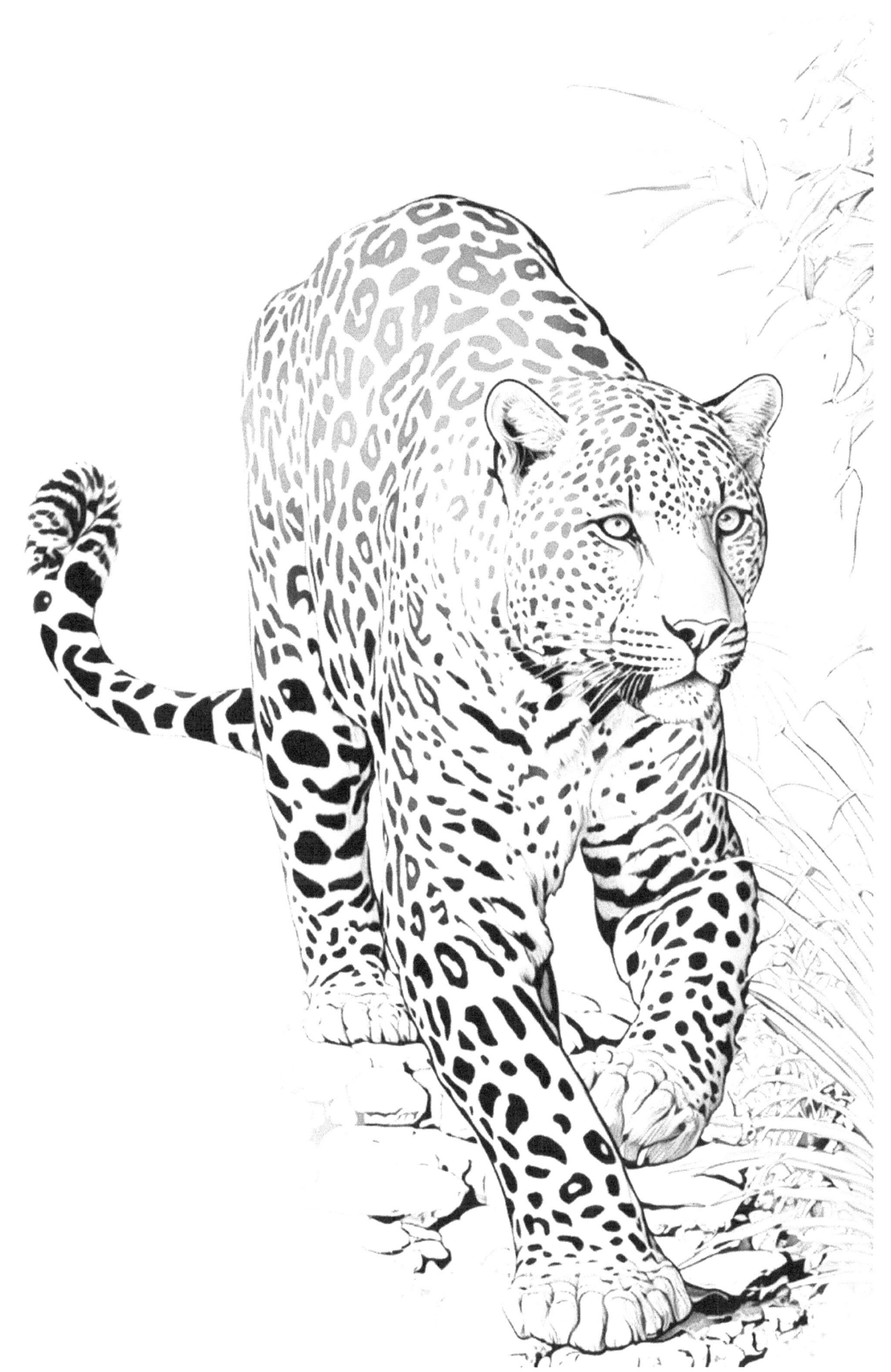

# Manatee

The manatee is a large aquatic mammal found in shallow coastal waters and rivers. It is a herbivorous animal that feeds mainly on aquatic plants. Manatees are slow-moving animals and are known for their gentle nature. They are also an endangered species due to habitat loss and hunting.

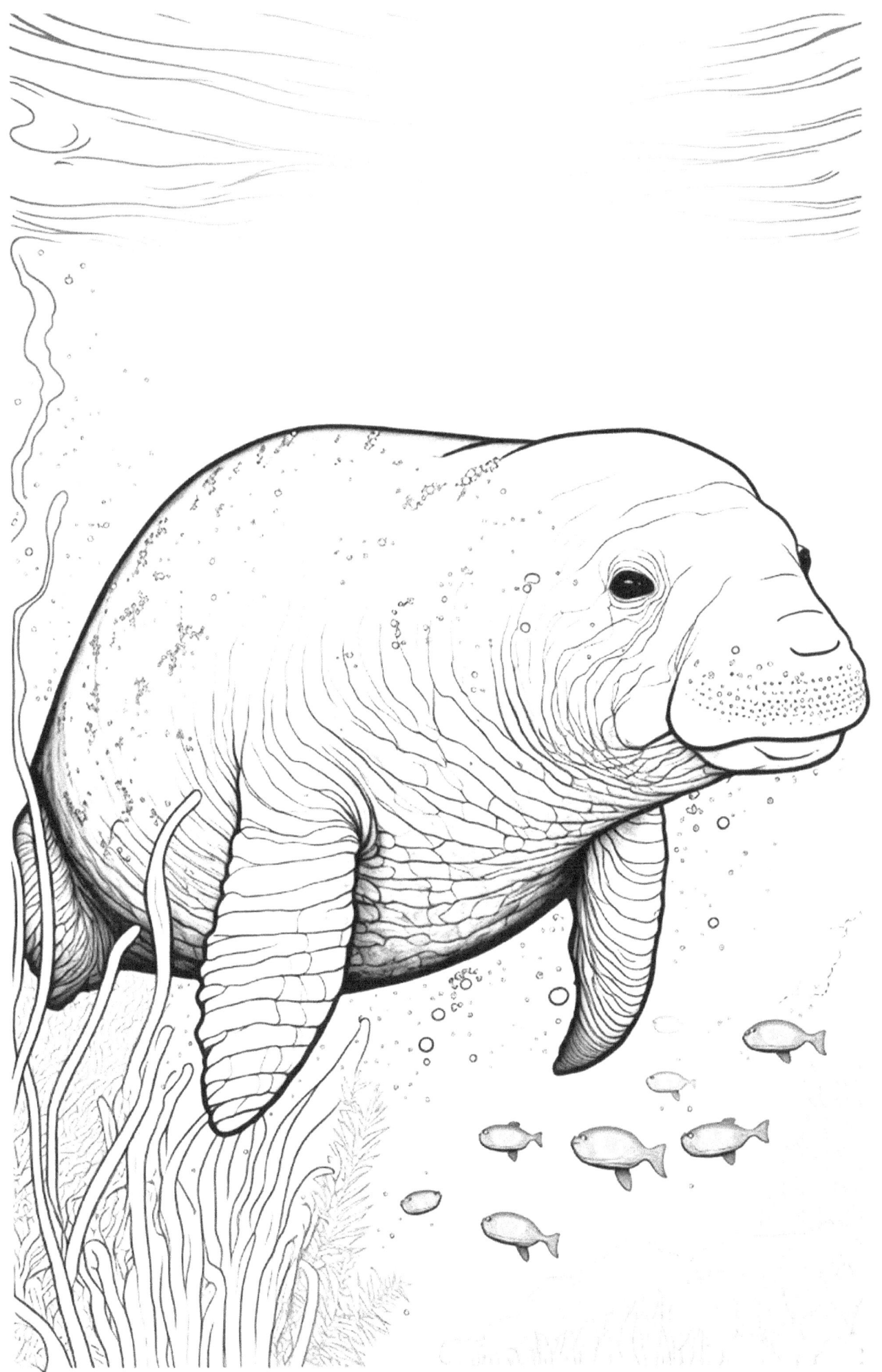

# Macaws

Macaws are large colorful birds belonging to the family *Psittacidae*.
They are native to Central and South America and are known for their bright plumage and strong beaks.
Macaws are social birds that live in flocks and feed on fruits, nuts, seeds, and insects.
Some macaw species are threatened due to habitat loss and capture for the pet trade.

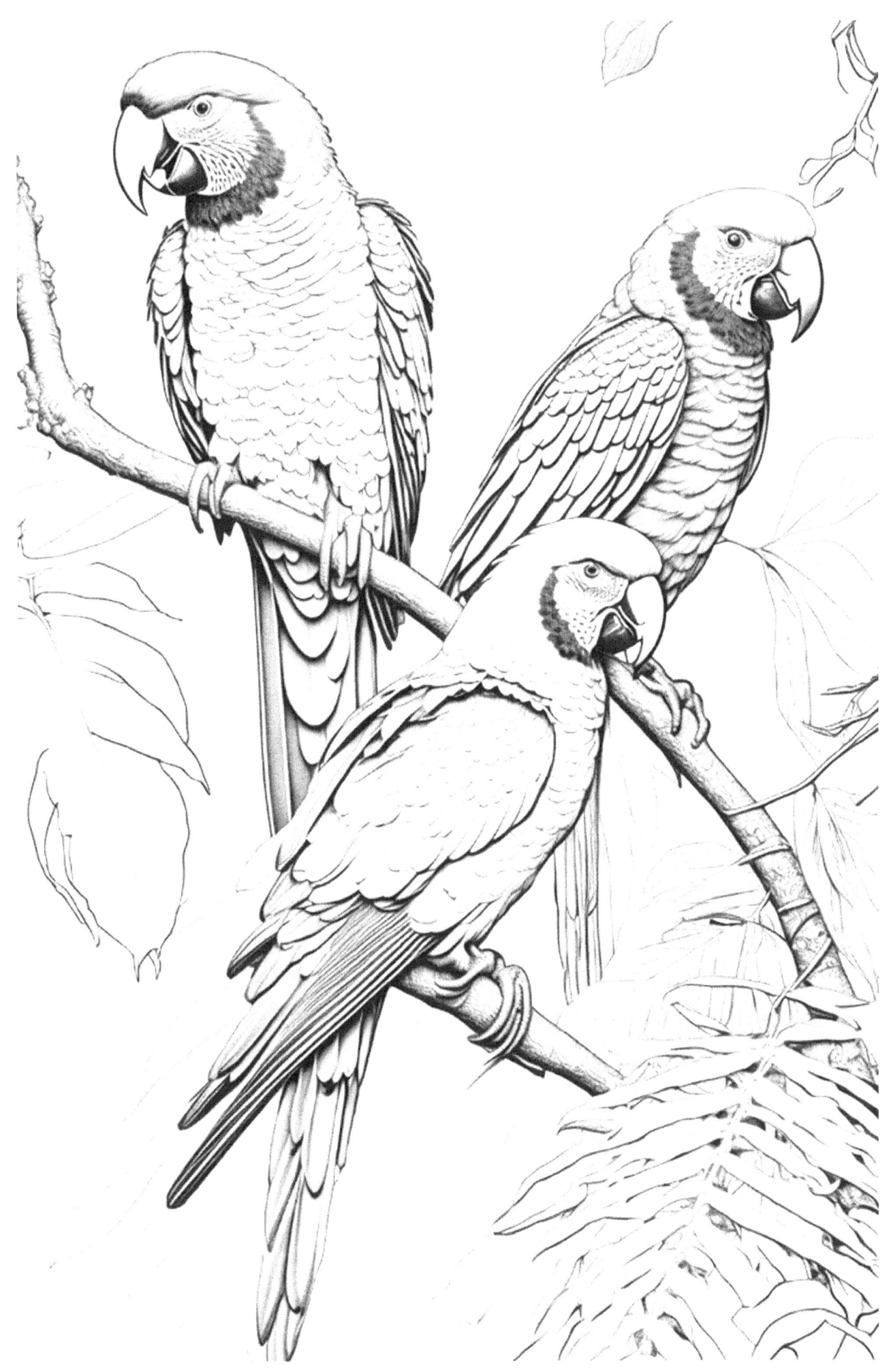

# Ocelot

The ocelot is a medium-sized wildcat native to the Americas. It is a carnivorous animal that feeds on a variety of prey, including rodents, rabbits, birds, reptiles and fish. The ocelot is a solitary animal that is active mainly at night.
It is also an excellent climber and can be found in a variety of habitats, including forests, grasslands and wetlands.

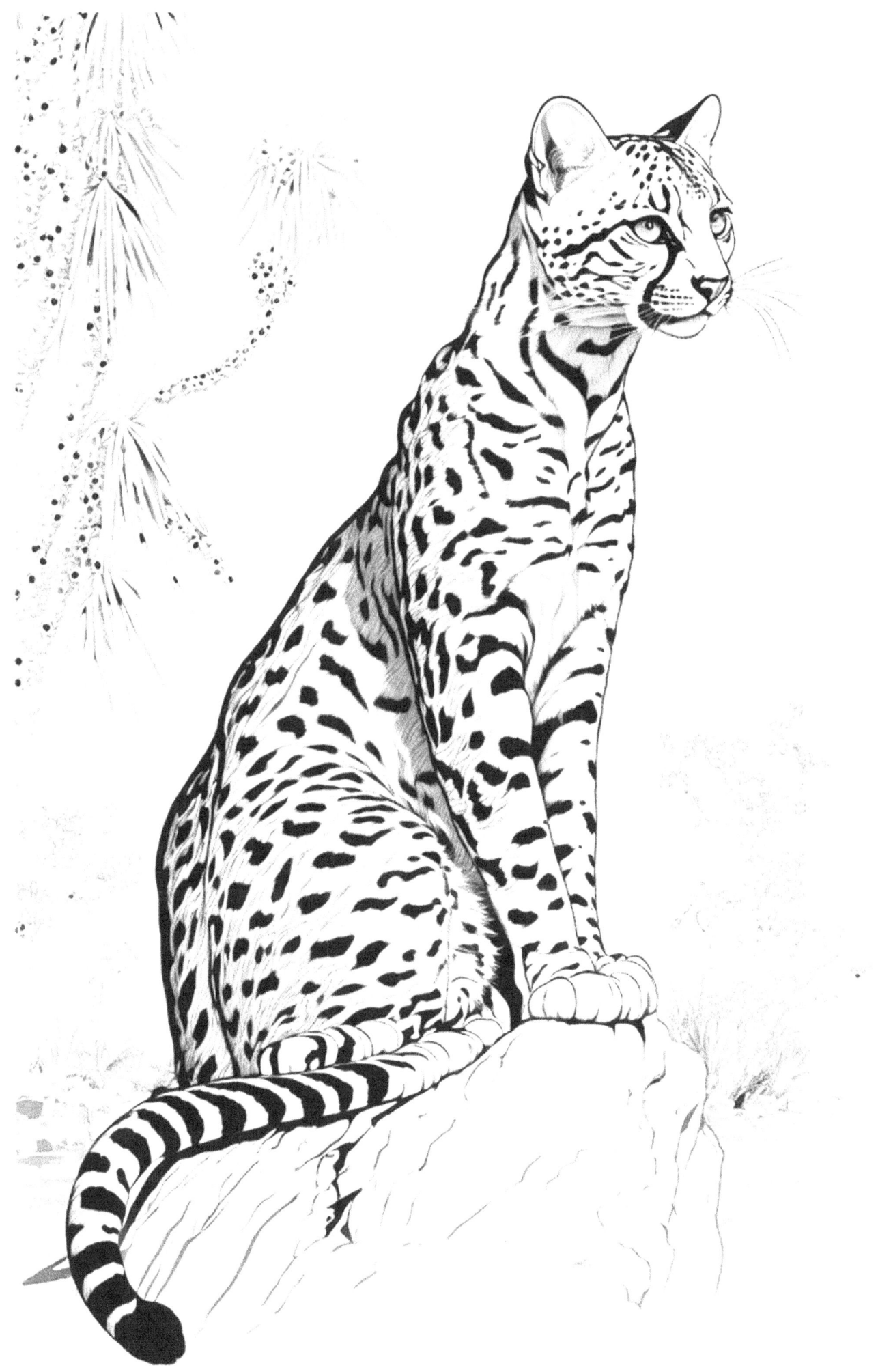

# Armadillo

The armadillo is a small mammal native to the Americas. It is known for its distinctive armor-like shell and long claws used for digging.

Armadillos are omnivorous animals that feed on insects, small vertebrates, fruits, and carrion.

They are also known for their ability to curl into a ball when threatened.

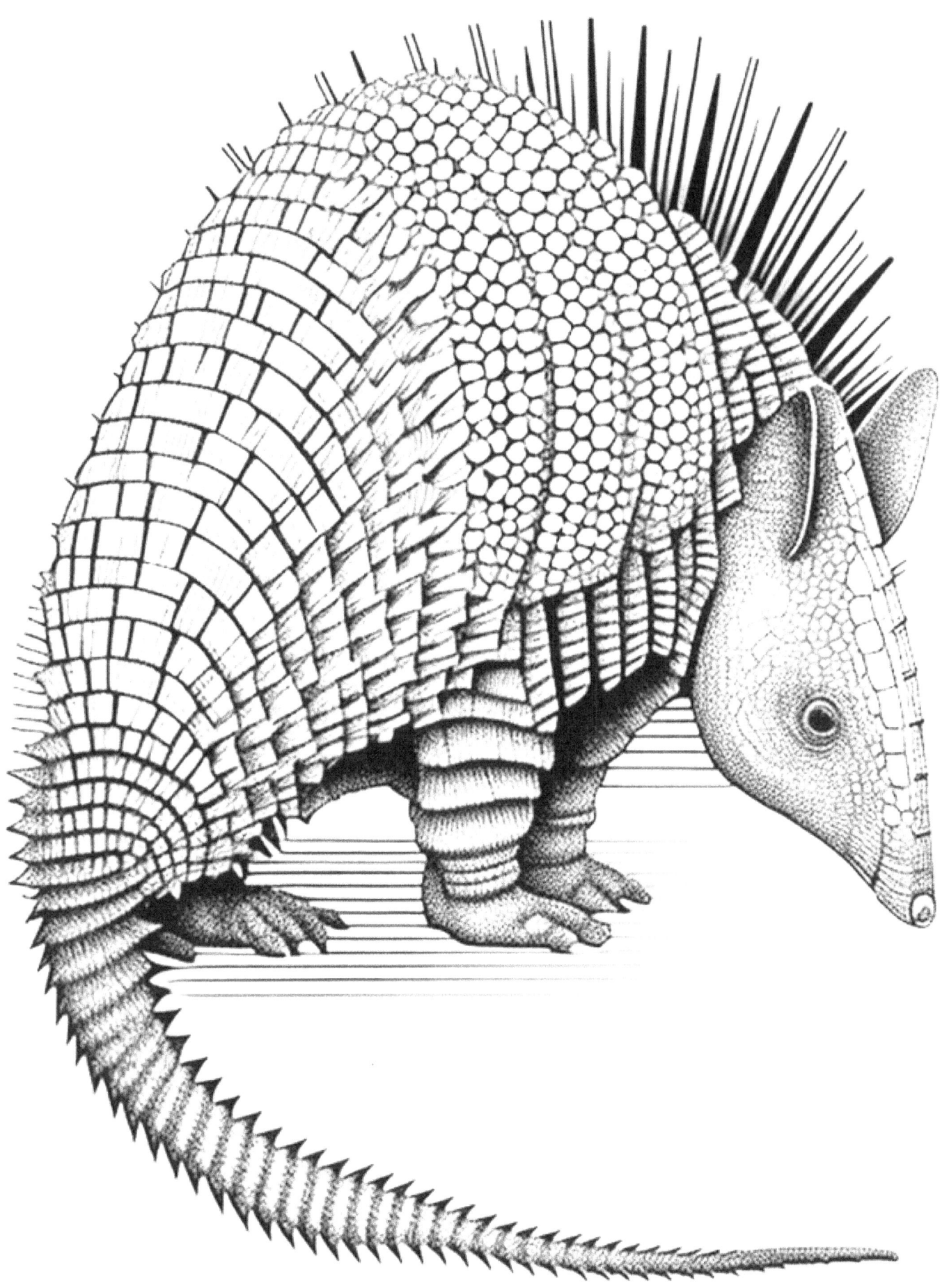

# Eagles

Eagles are large birds of prey belonging to the *Accipitridae* family.
They are found on every continent except Antarctica and are known for their sharp claws and curved beaks.
Eagles are carnivorous animals that feed on a variety of prey, including mammals, birds, reptiles, and fish.
They are also top predators and play an important role in maintaining the balance of their ecosystem.

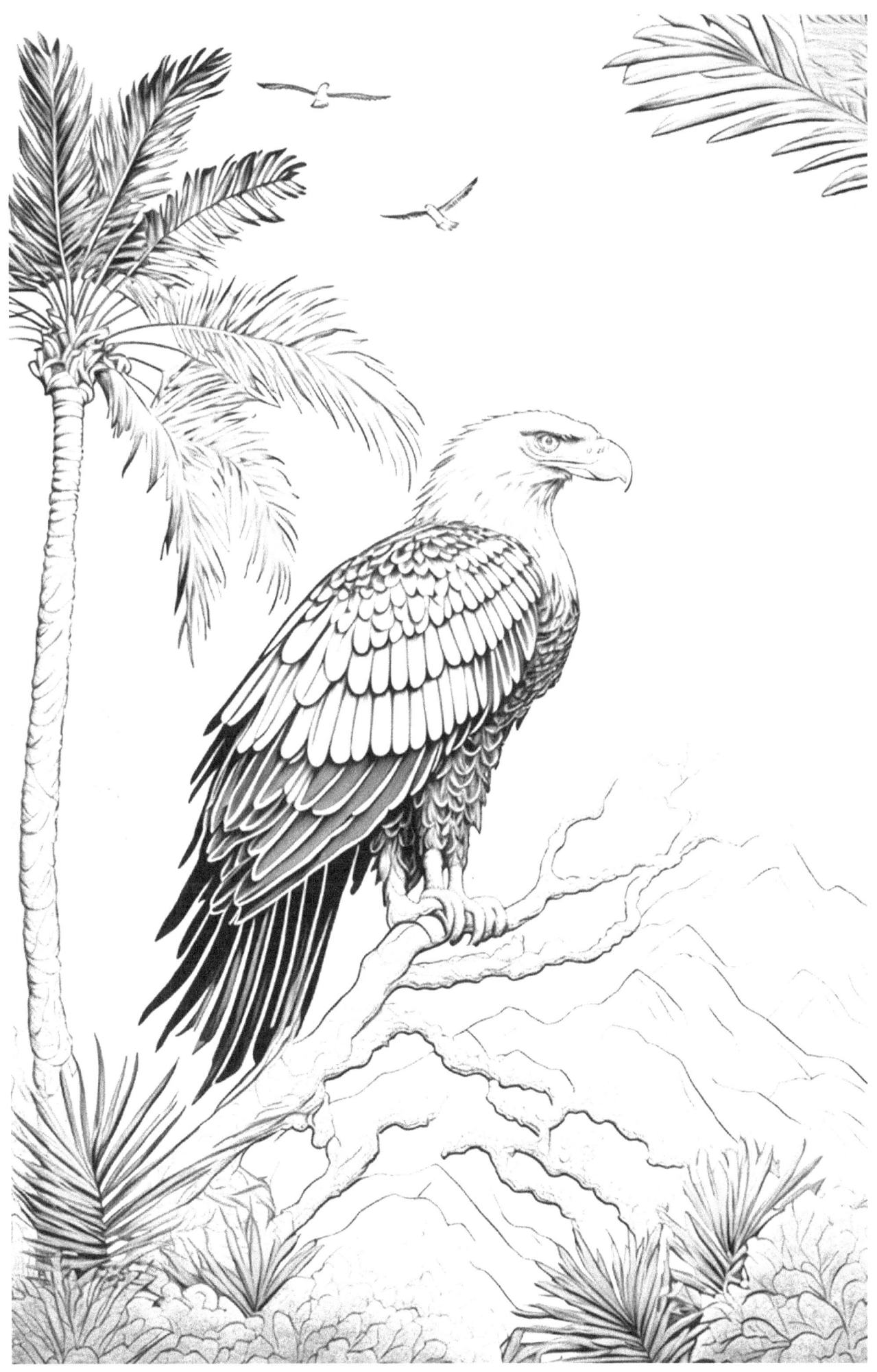

# Boa constrictor

Boa constrictors are large non-venomous snakes belonging to the family *Boidae*. They are found in the Americas and known for their distinctive patterns and ability to constrict their prey.

Boa constrictors are carnivorous animals that feed on a variety of animals, including mammals, birds, reptiles, and amphibians. They are also excellent climbers and can be found in a variety of habitats.

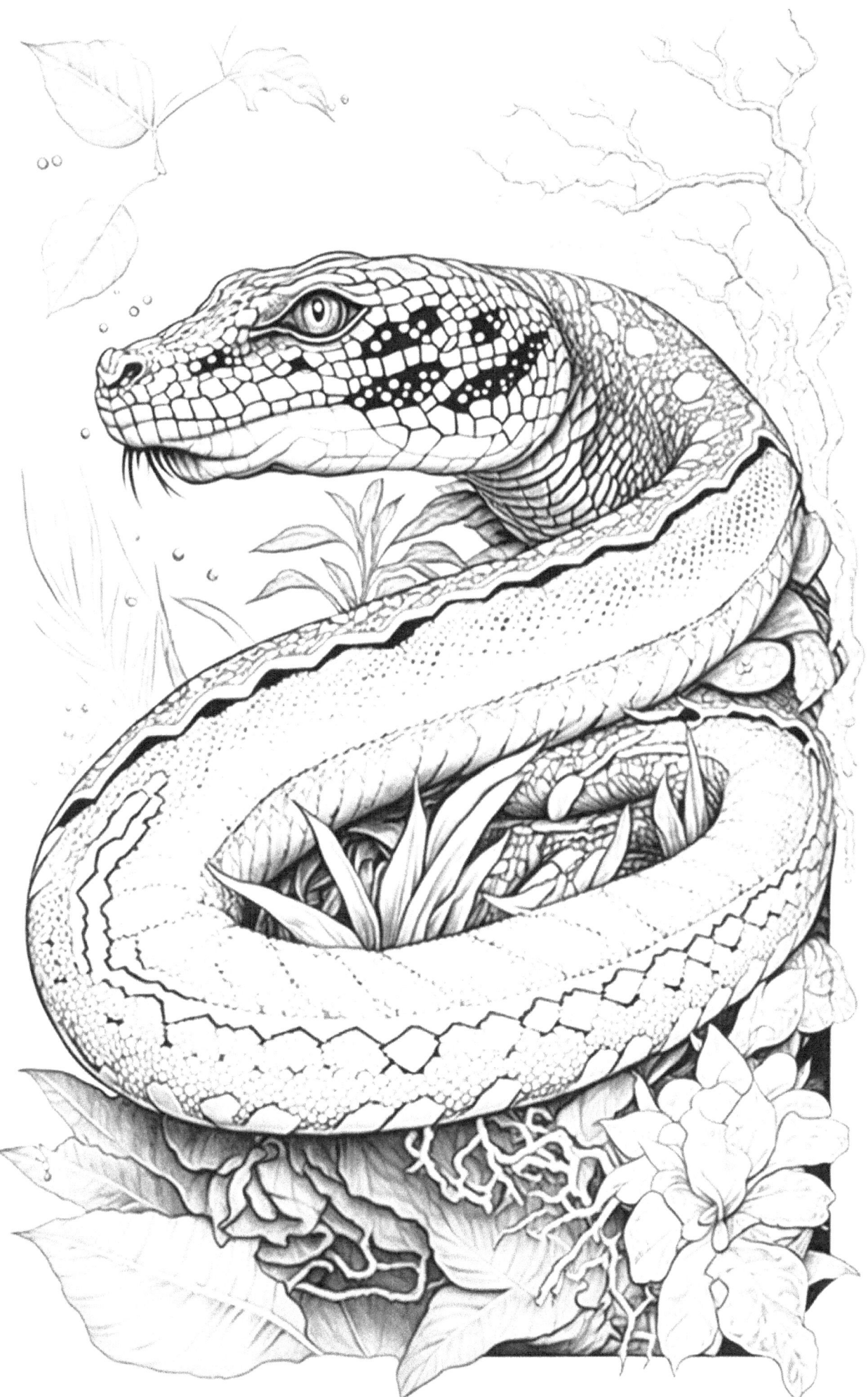

# Temperate Forest

It is formed by four basic strata of vegetation, namely:

Creeping: composed of lichens and mosses;

Herbaceous: composed of grasses and herbs that bloom in the spring;

Shrub: composed of trees of three to five meters, such as the wild mulberry;

Arboreal: composed of large trees, such as oak and maple.

The fall of leaves in late autumn and early winter is one of the main characteristics of temperate forests.
The goal is to reduce the metabolism of the plant as an important defense strategy, since winters are harsh and can last up to three months. They are biomes that have four well-defined seasons.
The flora is composed of large trees and broad leaves.

# Wolves

Wolves have a great sense of smell and hearing, which allows them to search for their prey and enables communication between them. They also possess good eyesight, allowing them to hunt successfully at night.

They are very territorialistic and delimit their space by marking with urine, feces or impregnating the ground with their smell.

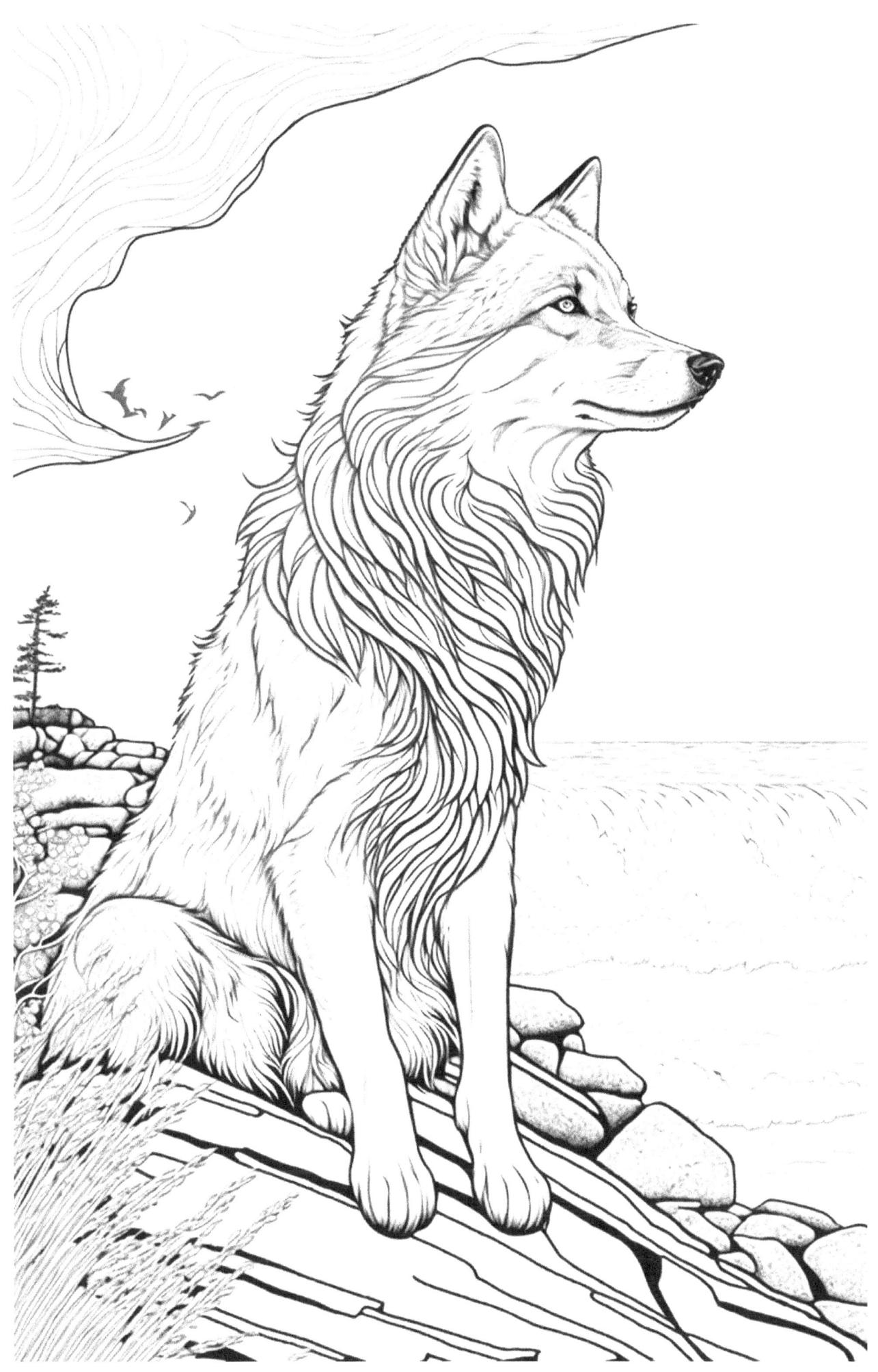

# Deer

Deer are placental mammals that form the *deer* family. The main feature is the horns; these bony structures are present in all deer except the Chinese water deer (*Hydropotes inermis inermis*).
Another characteristic of horns is that only males have them, except in the case of the Rangifer species, where both sexes have horns.

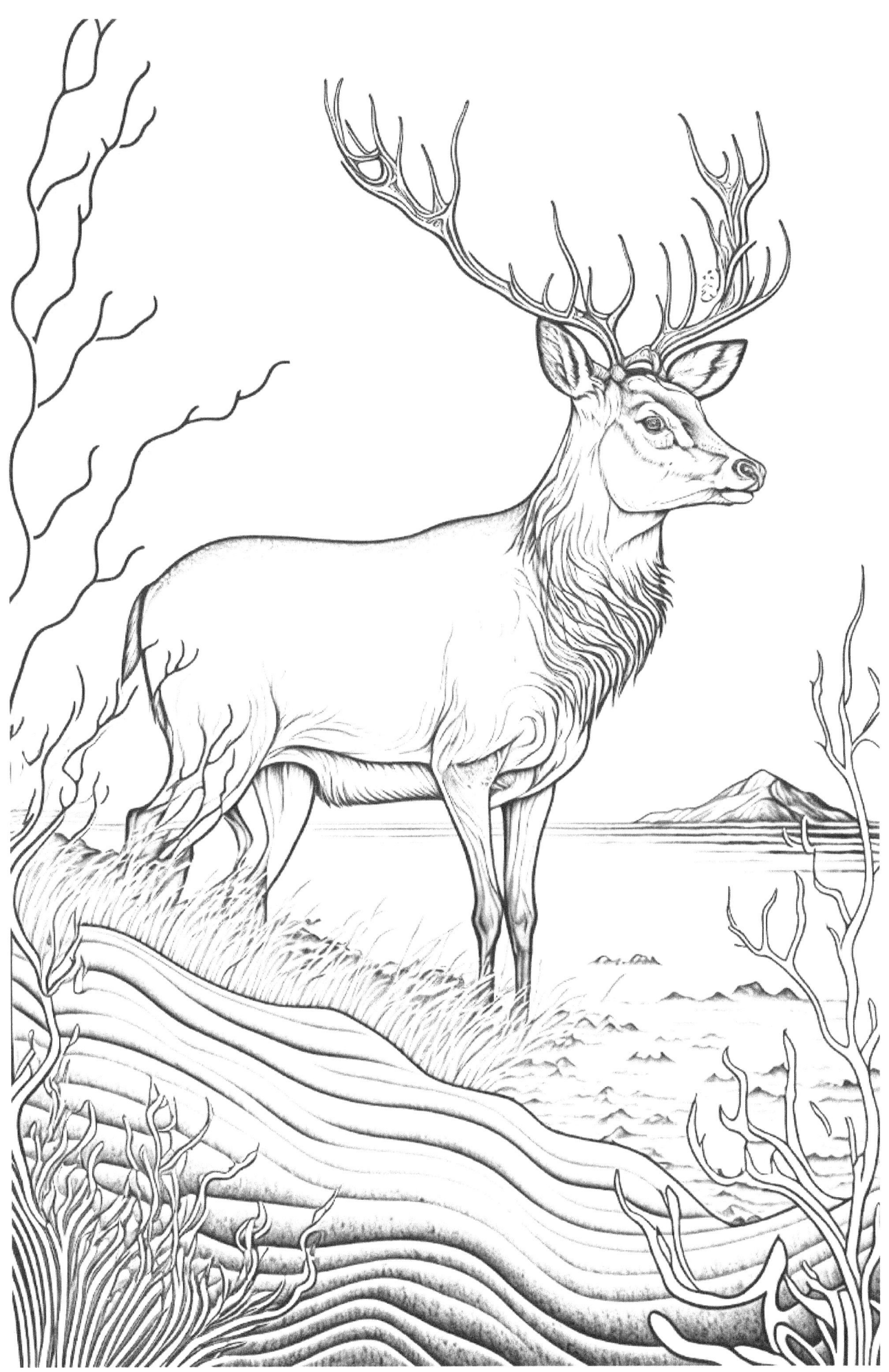

# Bats

Bats are small mammals, the largest individuals belong to a family of giant bats and can have up to 1.7 meters in wingspan and weigh about 1.2 kg. They usually have small eyes, large ears and sharp teeth. Bats have some characteristics common to other mammals such as the body covered by hair, and the density of these hairs varies according to the species, as well as the coloration, which usually varies between brown and grayish brown.

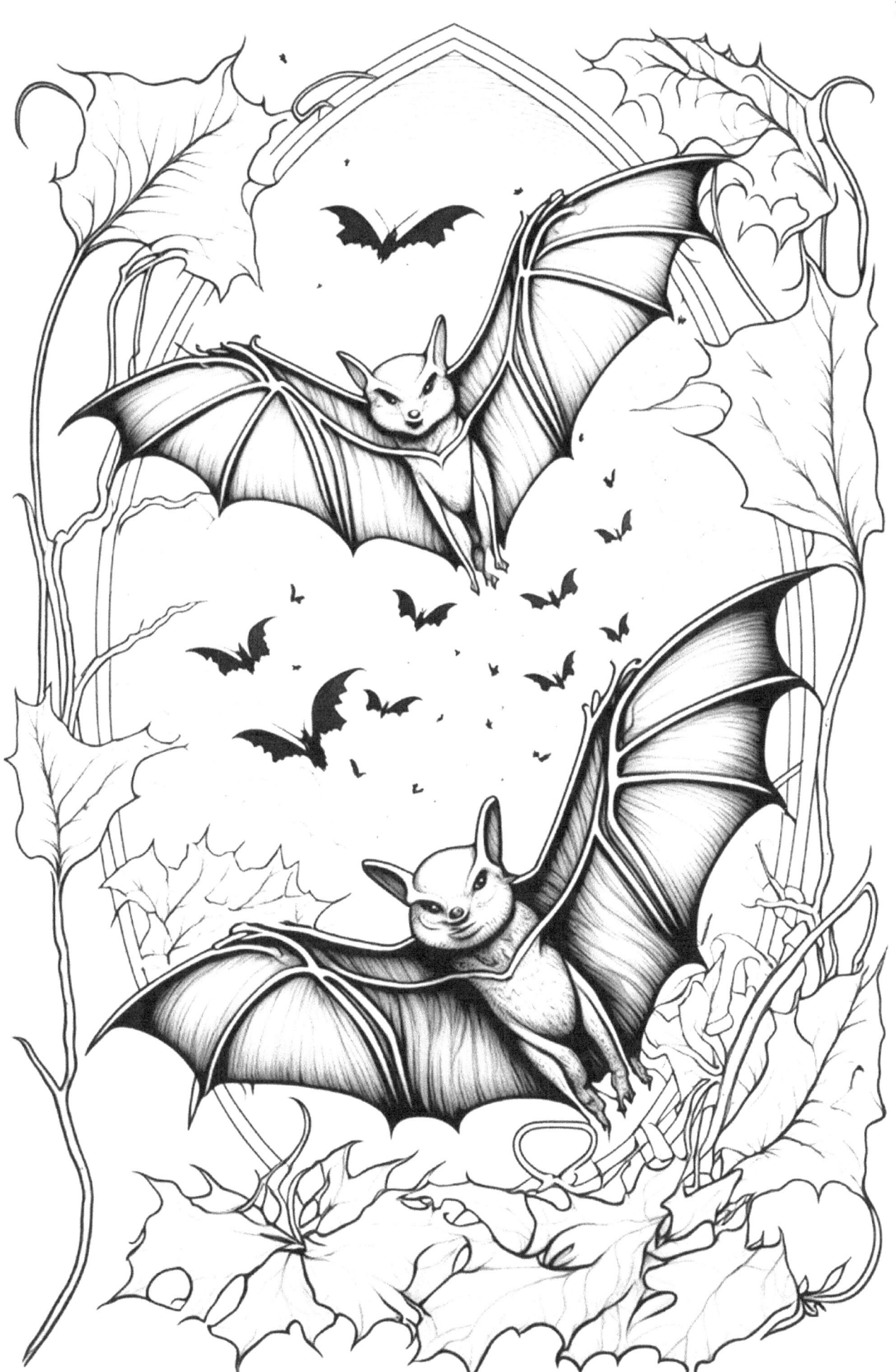

# Owls

Owls are a group of birds that have some peculiar features such as a flattened face, forward-facing eyes, a curved and strong beak. They are animals that have a wide variety of size, there are small species, with about 60 g and others that can weigh up to more than 1 kg.
The coloration of the feathers varies from one species to another, but most have brown, white or gray feathers.

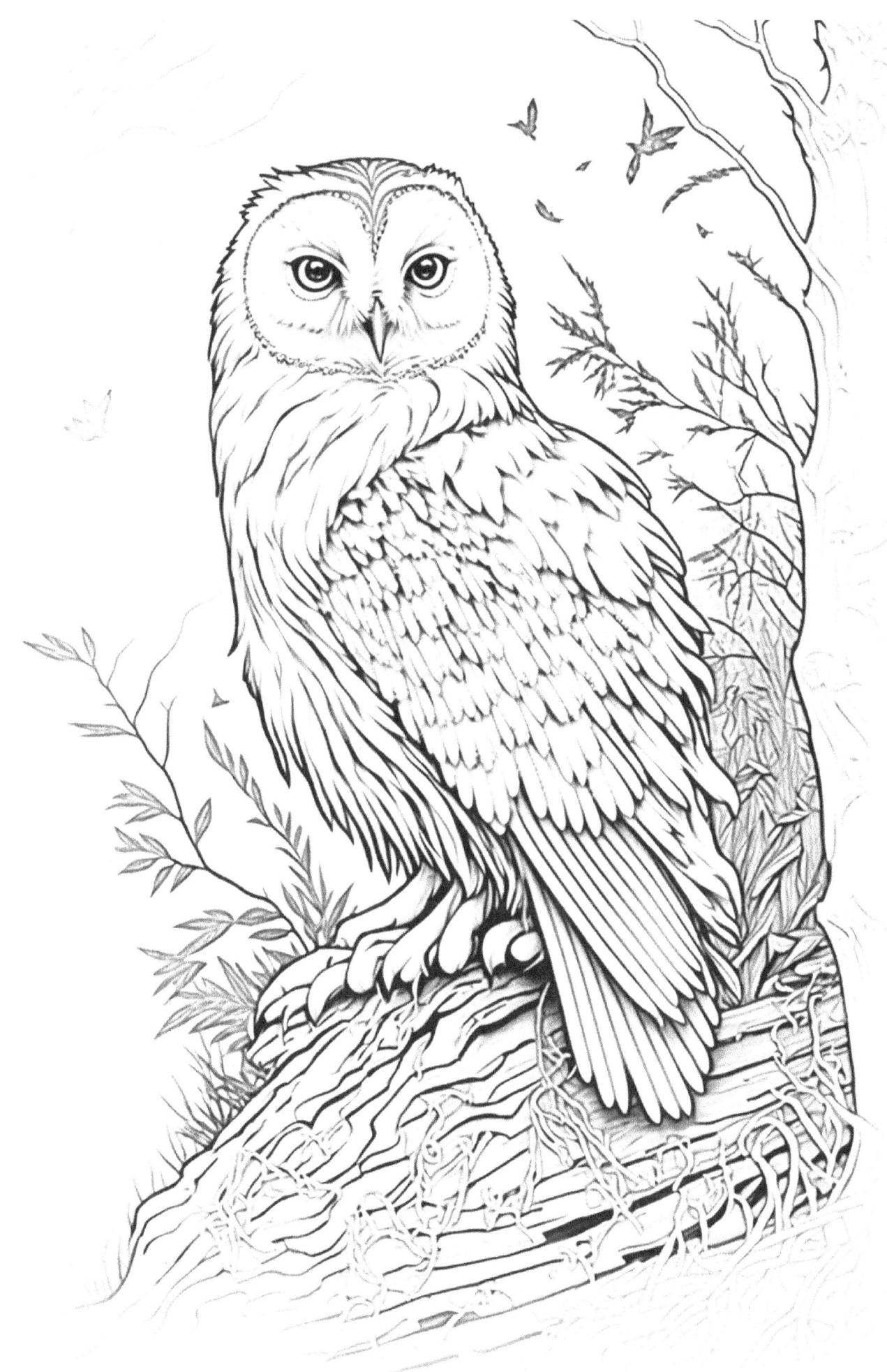

# Koala

The body of the koala is egg-shaped and has no tail, a very peculiar feature of this species. His face is wide, with large eyes, round and hairy ears.
Koalas exhibit a remarkable sexual dimorphism, which facilitates the differentiation of males and females. Males are usually longer than females, with a larger head and nose. In addition, its chest is wide and has a brown color.

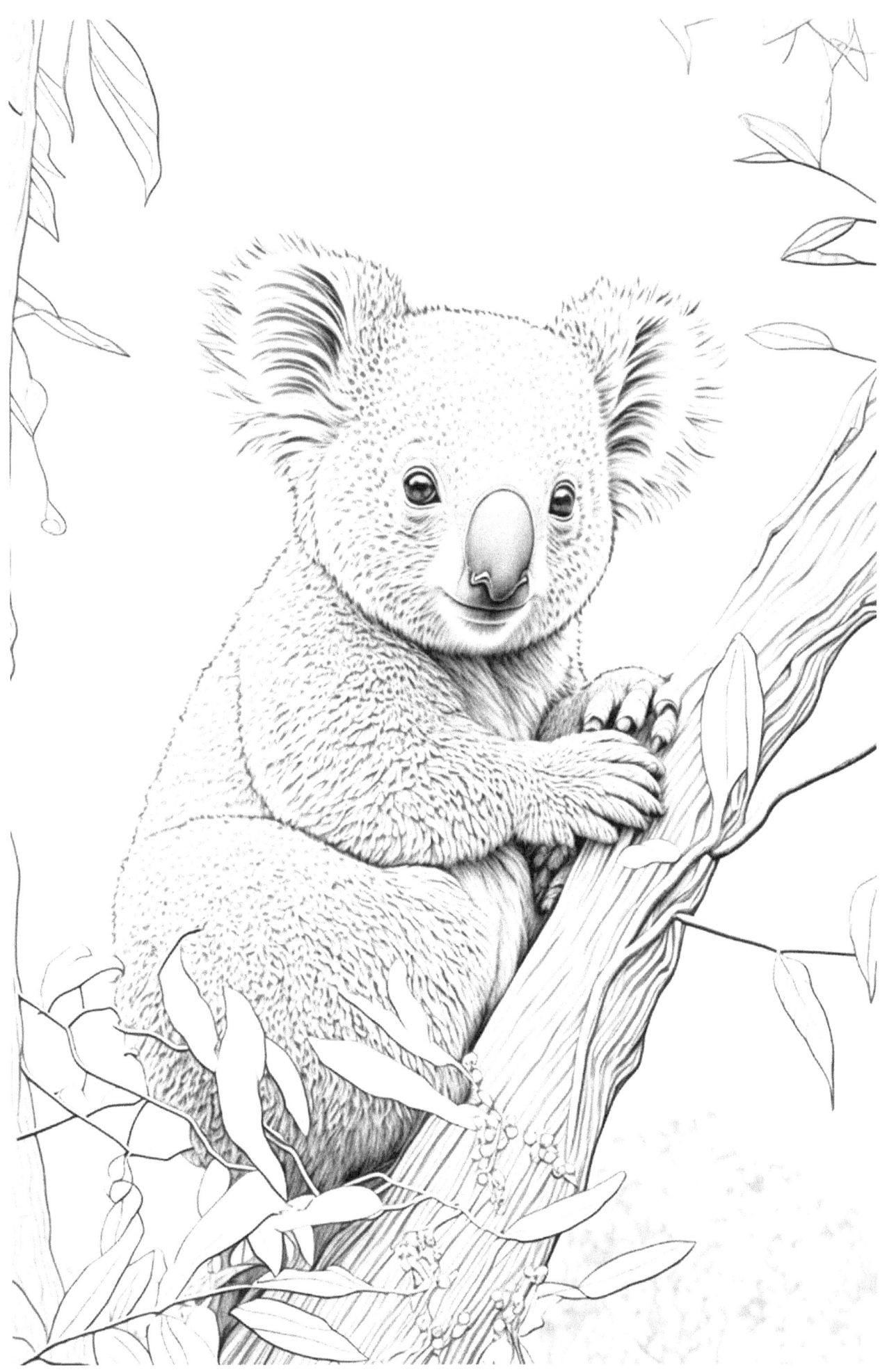

# Kangaroo

Kangaroos are animals that are part of the *macropodidae* family, a family that gets its name due to the large feet of its representatives.
Kangaroos, in addition to their large feet, have large, well-developed hind legs.
The strong legs of this animal are essential to ensure a proper jump.

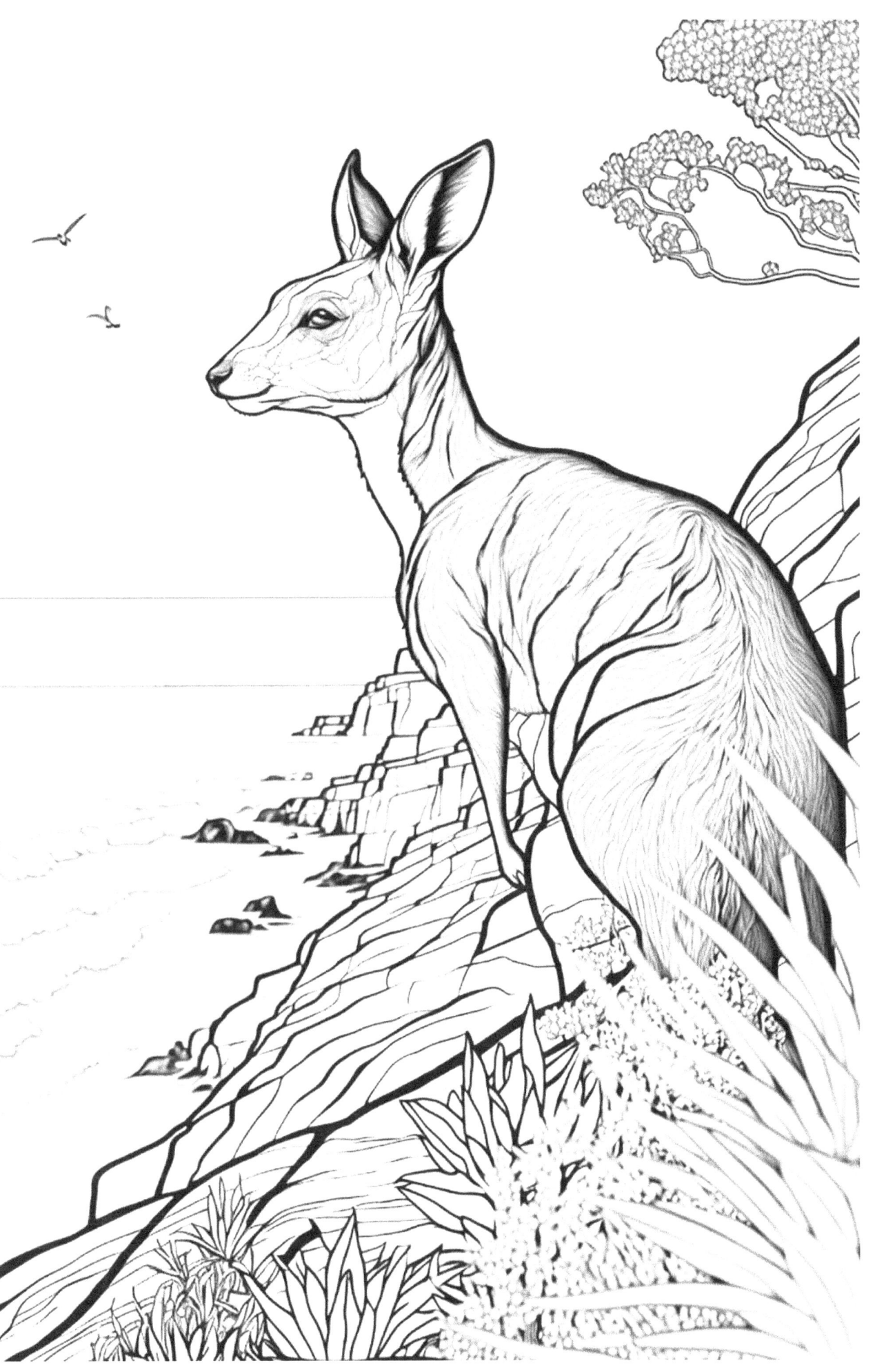

# Giant panda

Giant pandas are mammals that live in the forests of China.
They have a very characteristic coat pattern, these being easily recognized from their white hair and black spots around the eyes, ears, limbs and shoulders. These animals weigh between 75 and 160 kg and can reach more than 1.20 m in height.

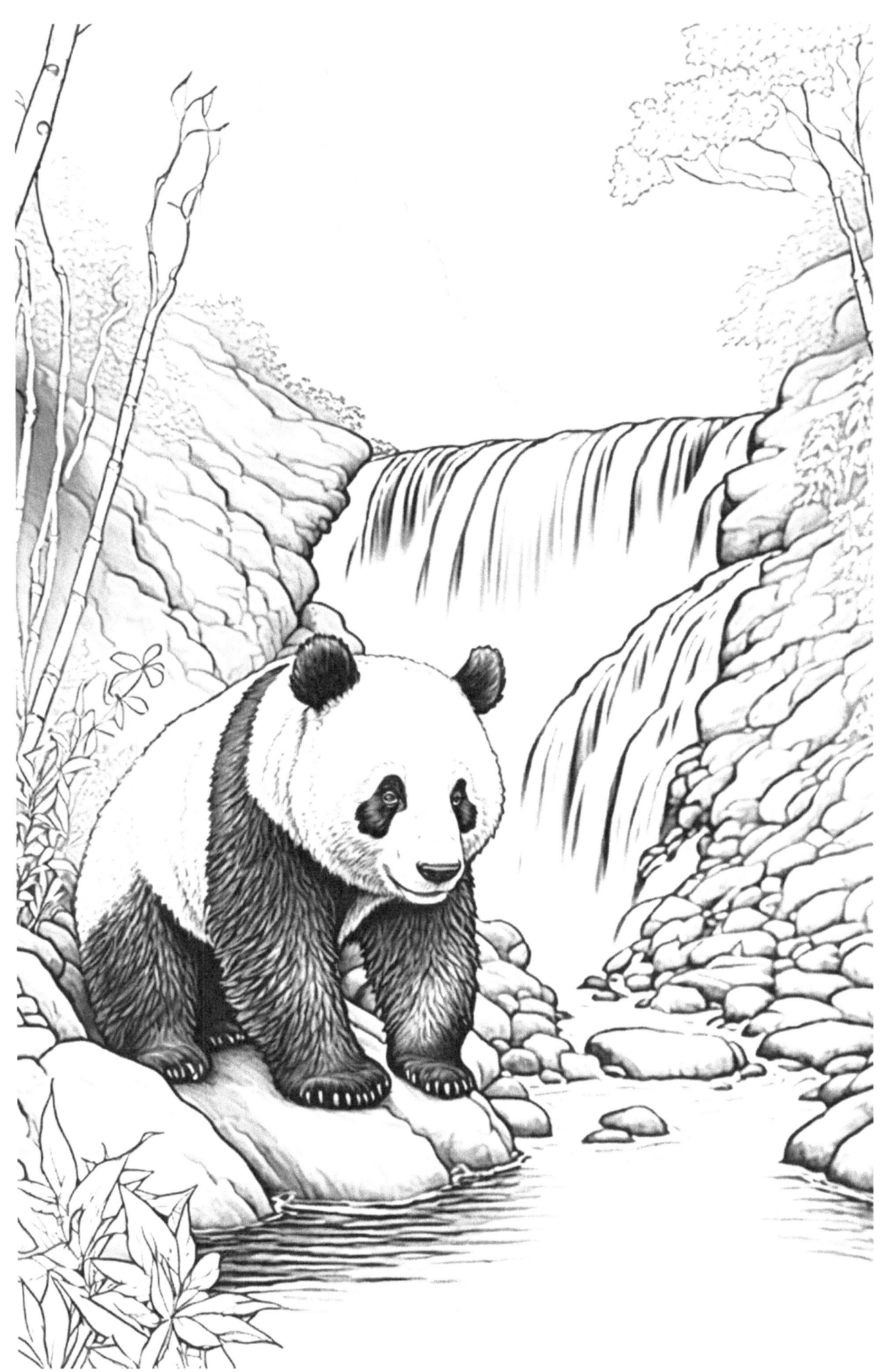

# Boreal Forest

It is a biome made up of the Taiga — also called the Conifera. This type of vegetation is formed mainly by pines, cypresses, firs, spruces and larch. These trees are tall, with straight trunks, cone-shaped canopies, thin needle-shaped leaves, and lined with a resin-like substance. Fundamental feature so that they do not accumulate snow and prevents moisture loss and freezing.

The fauna is also not rich in variety of species. It is a biome that presents cold and humid climate. It stretches across the cold regions of northern Russia, Scandinavia and Canada, above latitude 50° North - with very cold climates and icy soil. The animals that live in the boreal forest are adapted to the cold and humid climate, with snow at least during the middle of the year and minimum temperature of -50°C and special characteristics that help them survive in such a hostile environment.

# Squirrels

Squirrels are small rodents with long, hairy tails. They have sharp, strong teeth, which they use to gnaw nuts and seeds. They are agile and fast animals, able to jump from tree to tree with ease. They are found in many parts of the world and live in forests, parks and gardens.

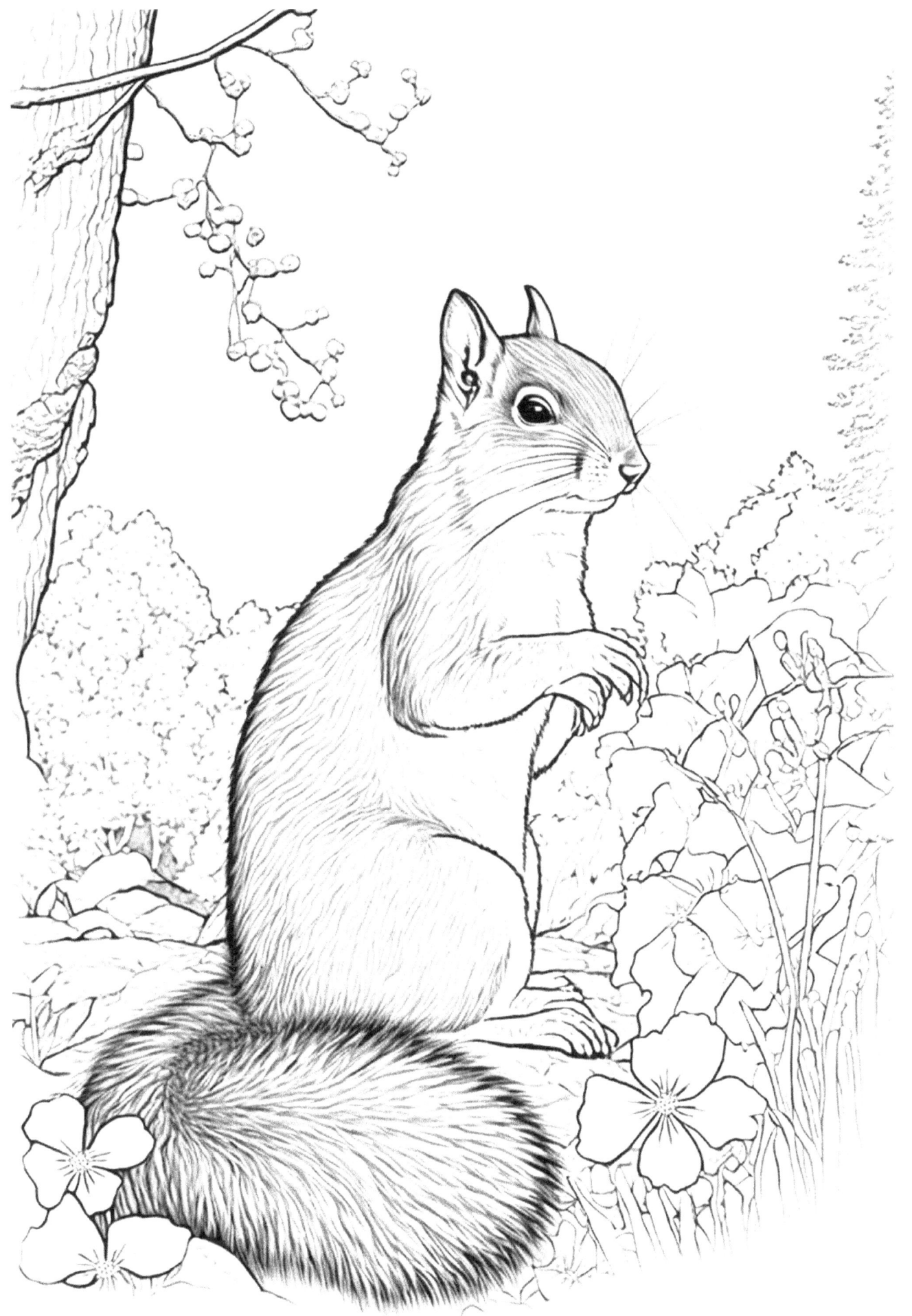

# Reindeer

Reindeer are mammals of the deer family, found in the cold regions of the northern hemisphere. They have thick coats to protect themselves from the cold and large, branching horns. Reindeer are social animals that live in groups and feed mainly on lichens, mosses and leaves.

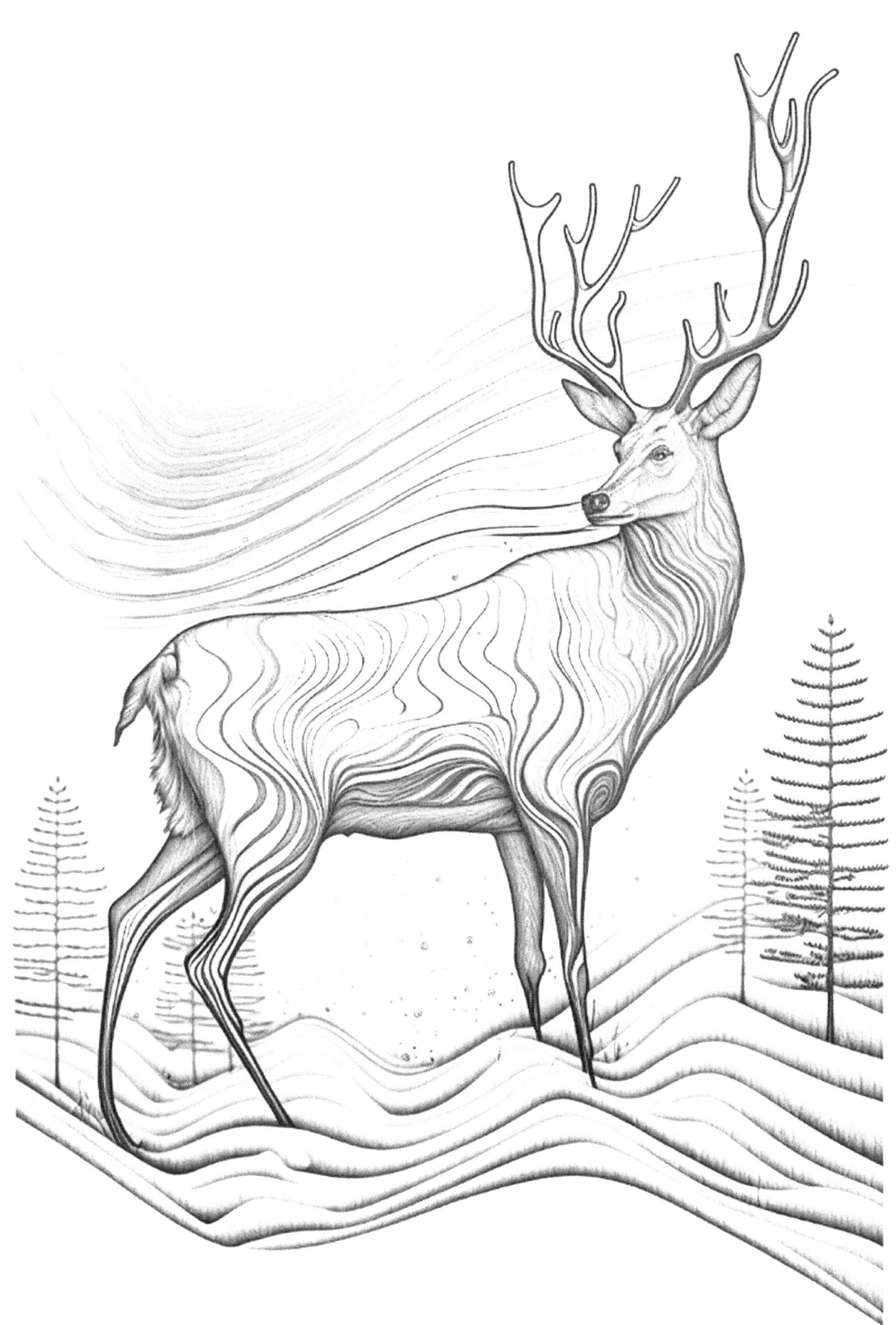

# Fox

Foxes are carnivorous mammals of the *canid* family. They have thick coats, usually reddish in color, and long, hairy tails. They are cunning and intelligent animals, able to adapt to different environments. They feed on small mammals, birds, insects and fruits.

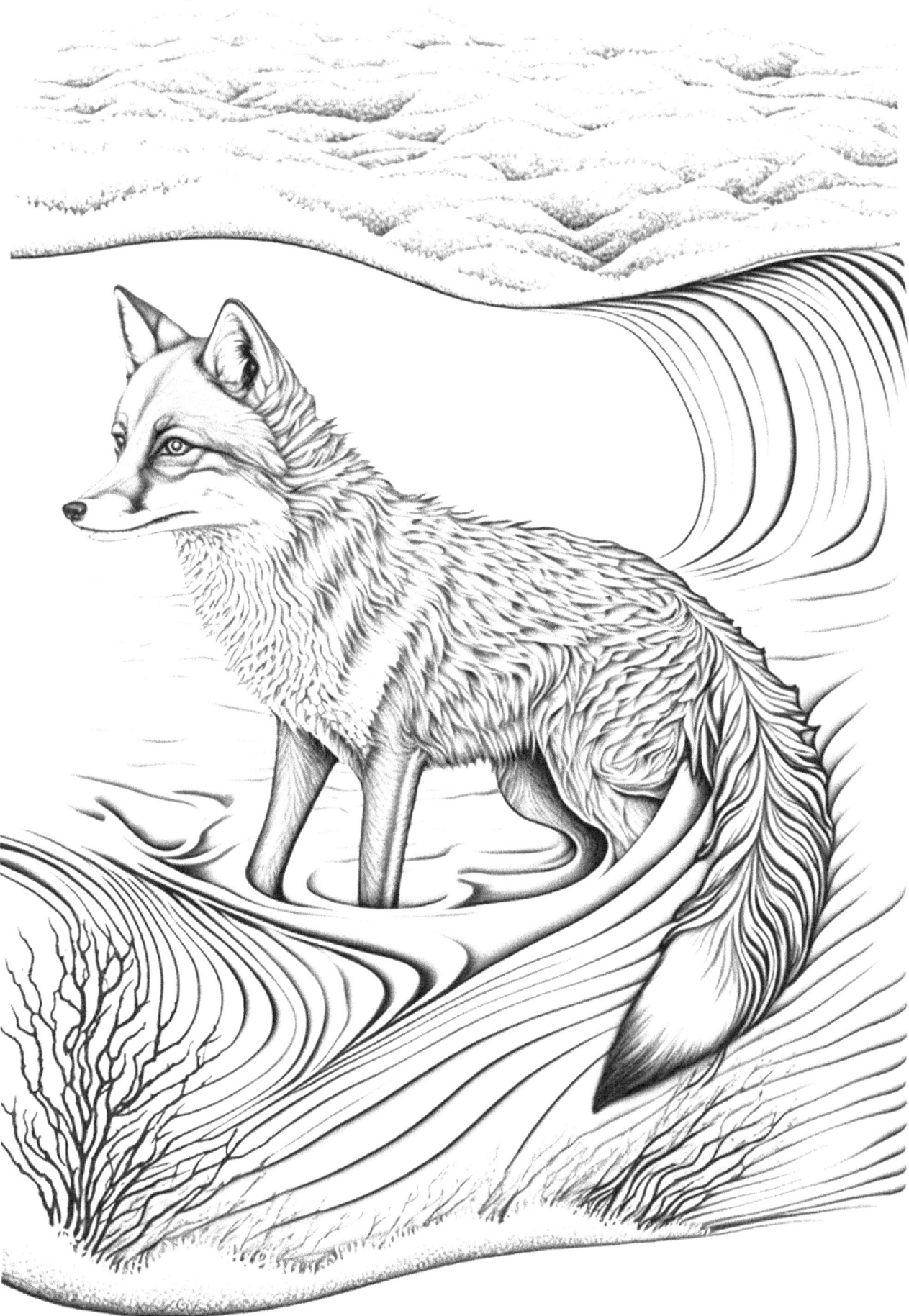

# Polar bear

Polar bears are carnivorous mammals found in the Arctic regions of the world. They have thick white coat to protect themselves from the cold and large paws with sharp claws to hunt their prey. They are excellent swimmers and feed mainly on seals.

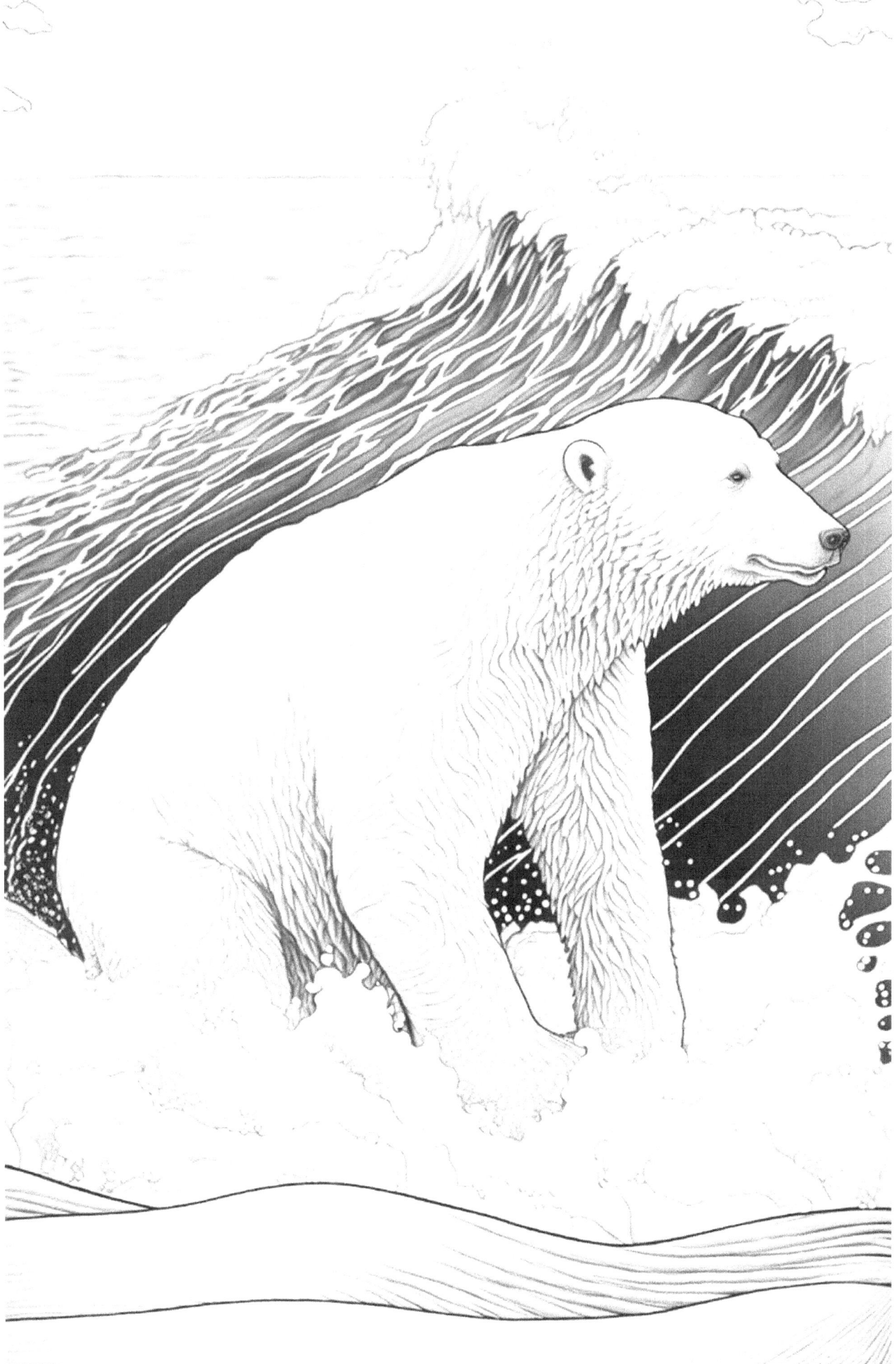

# Beaver

Beavers are semi-aquatic rodents found in North America and Europe. They have thick coat to protect themselves from the cold and sharp teeth to gnaw wood. Beavers have been known to build dams on rivers to create ponds where they can live. They feed mainly on tree bark, leaves, and aquatic plants.

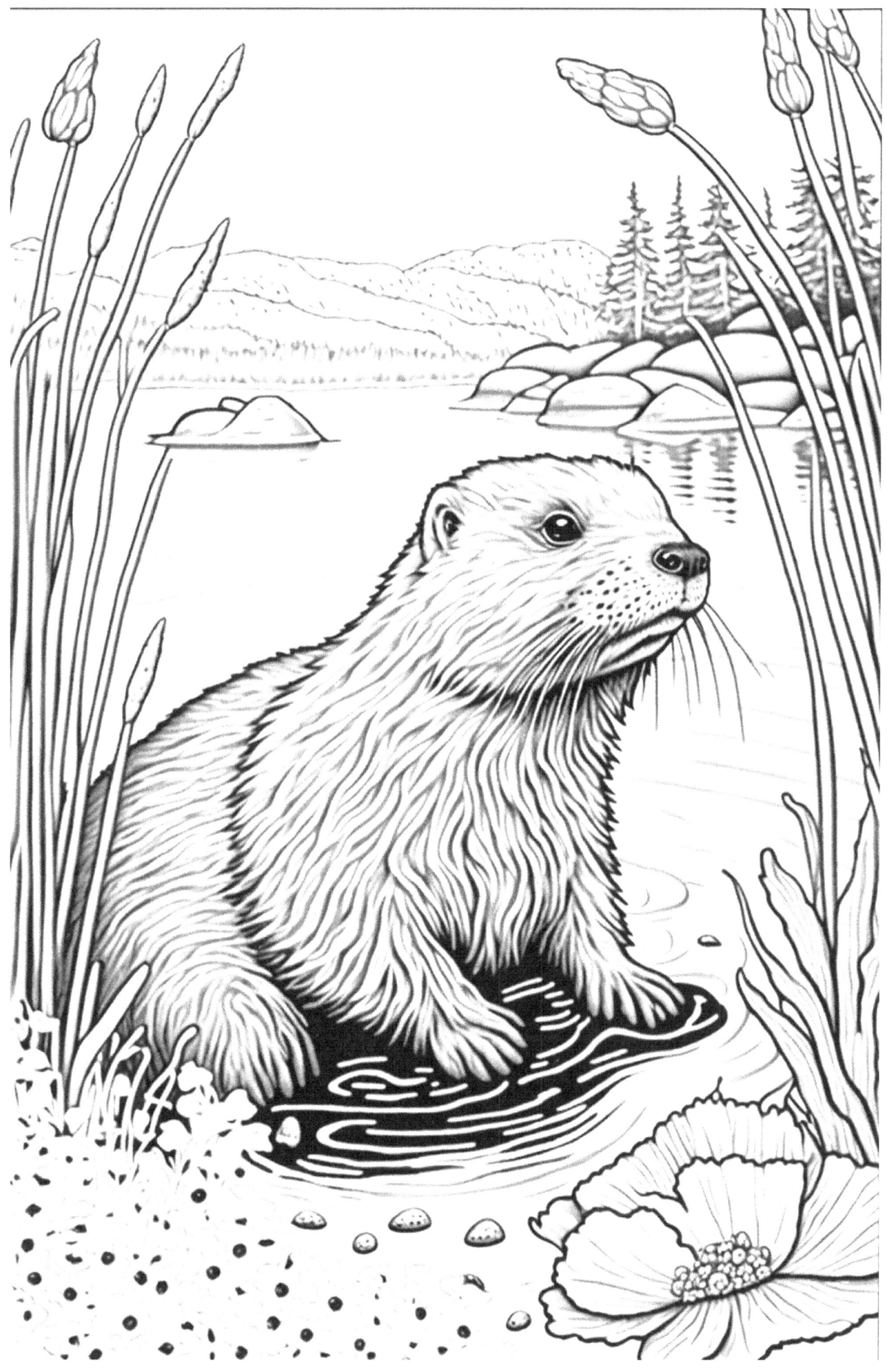

# Gray owl

The gray owl is a bird of prey found in North America, it has gray plumage with white spots and large, yellow eyes.
The gray owl is a nocturnal hunter that feeds primarily on small mammals such as rats and rabbits.

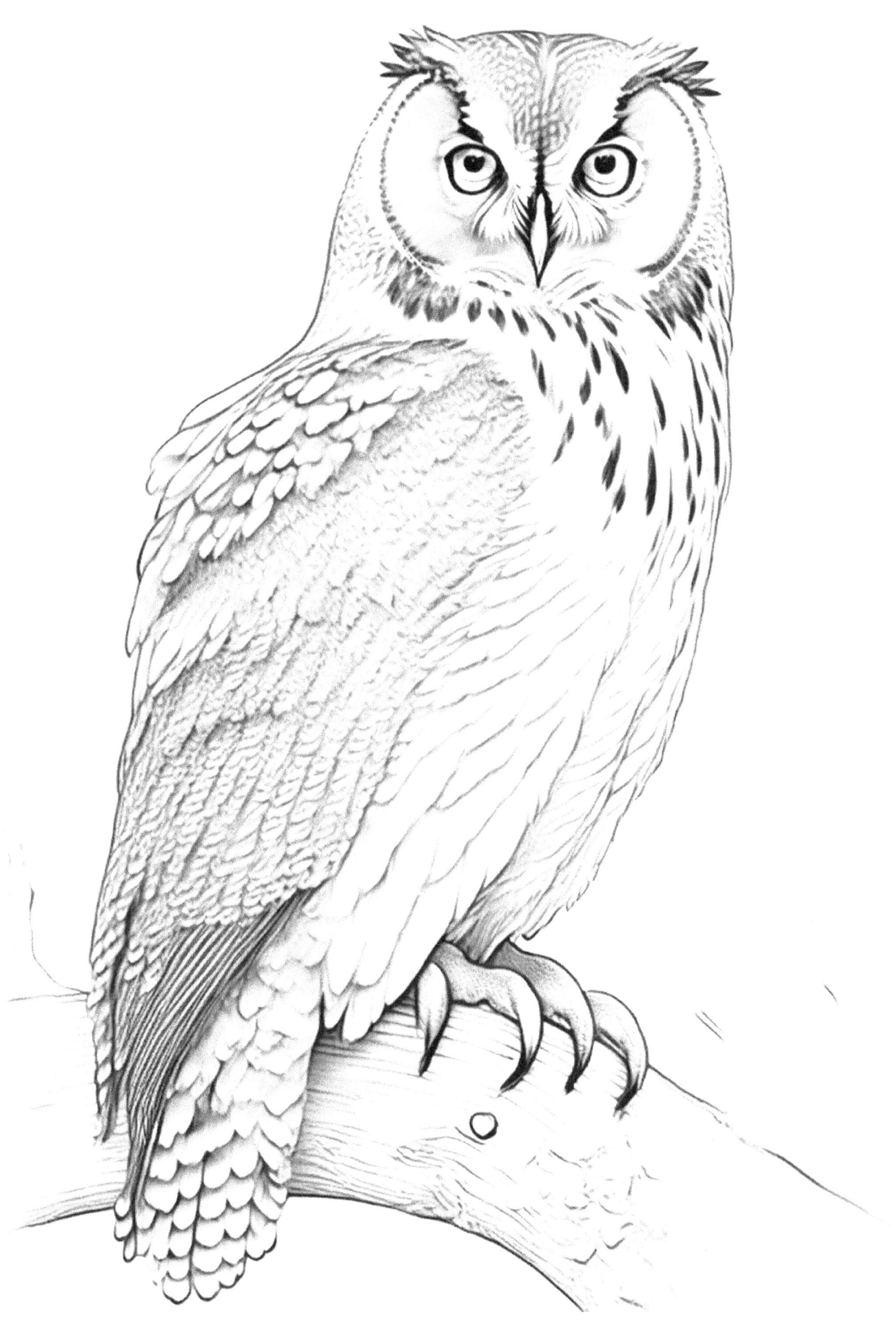

# American hare

The American hare is a mammal of the leporid family, found in North America. It has thick fur to protect itself from the cold and long ears to detect predators. The American hare is a fast animal that can run at speeds greater than 70 km/h. It feeds mainly on leaves, tree bark and shoots.

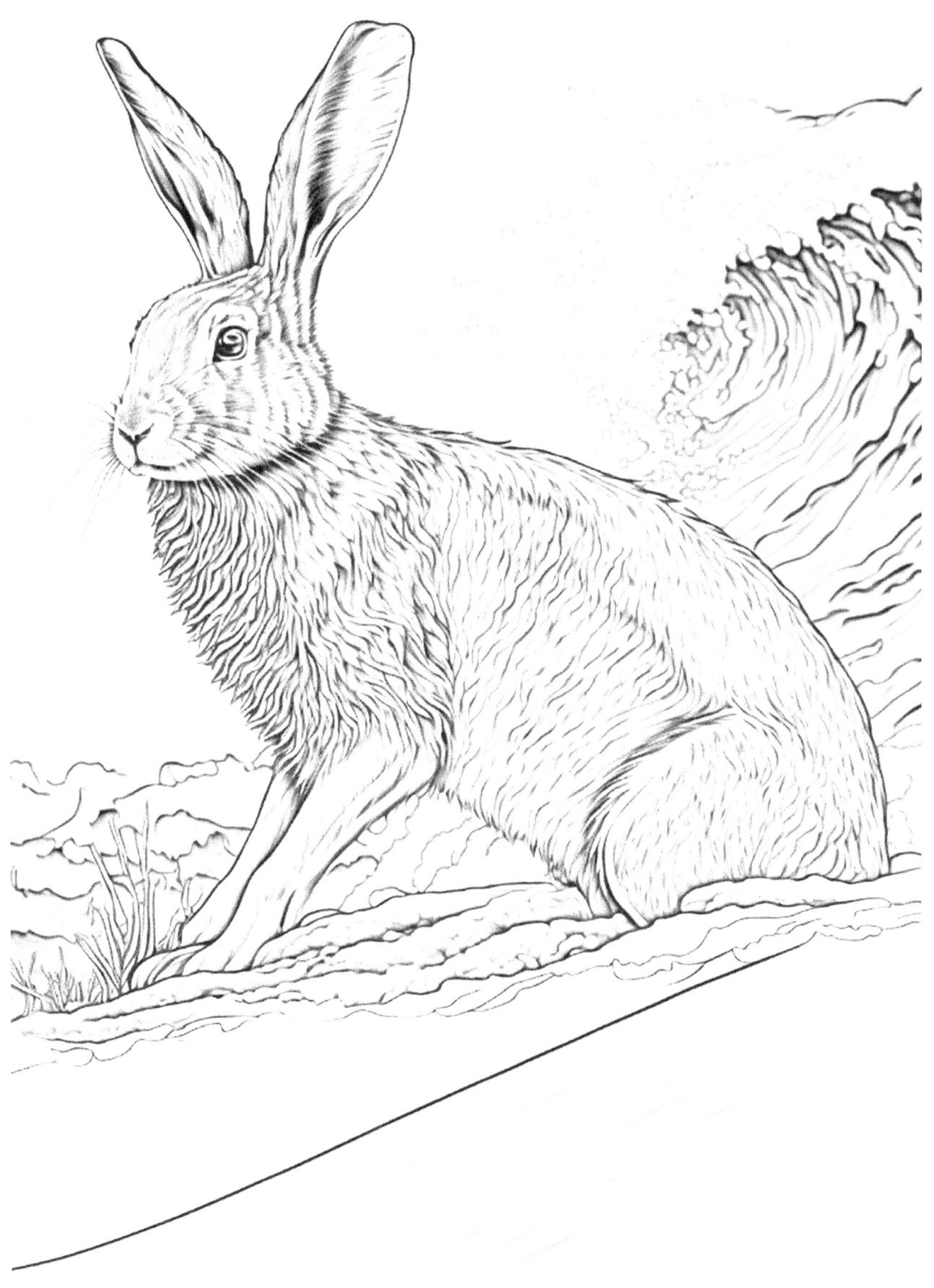